"Our past does not define our future."

*****

*Valuing Your*

# Value & Worth

*A Book of Inner Reflection*

**Harrison S. Mungal, Ph.D., PsyD**

Foreword by Jeff and Maj-Britt Edwards

**Valuing Your Value & Worth**

**Copyright © 2023 Harrison S. Mungal**

Printed in Canada

Contact author via email: info@agetoage.ca
www.agetoage.ca
www.harrisonmungal.com
www.harrisonmungalbooks.com
Facebook: Harrison Sharma Mungal
Twitter: HarrisonandKathleen @HKrelationships,
AgetoAge @agetoagec
LinkedIn: Harrison Mungal, Ph.D., PsyD
YouTube: Harrison Mungal
Phone: 905-533-1334

# **ABOUT THE AUTHOR**

Harrison holds two doctorate degrees, one in Clinical Psychology and the other in Philosophy in Social Work. He has two master's degrees, a master's degree in Social Work and a master's degree in Counselling. And a Bachelor's degree in Theology. He specializes in mental health, addictions, marriage and relationships, parenting and the family.

Harrison is considered one of the leading cognitive therapist workshop presenters. He wears many hats in supporting individuals, couples, families, and corporations. He has been a public speaker to over forty-two nations as a keynote speaker at conferences, seminars, and public events, as well as a speaker on several Radio and Television programs. He has written over thirty books. He is appreciated for the depth of his knowledge, great humour and passion for relationships, parenting, mental health, addictions, and other related life struggles.

Harrison utilizes a creative scientific-based approach to deliver compelling presentations that have granted him an excellent reputation. He has received several awards and recognitions from local police, mayors, community leaders, managers and directors, and families. He provides training and consultations to various community partners, including psychiatrists, medical doctors, social workers, nurses, police officers, firefighters and senior management teams.

Harrison has been involved in cognitive research to support individuals with addictions, psychosis, anxiety, and depression. He spearheaded several research studies on various themes, including music therapy and schizophrenia, vaccinations for children under six years old, substance abuse and addiction in the food service industry, and Thought Developmental Practice (TDP). His research on TDP with outpatient provided diversion methods to support substance abuse and addictions, anxiety, and depression under the supervision of the chief of psychiatry, Dr. David Koczerginski.

Harrison has over twenty-one years of professional experience working with diverse populations, including seventeen years in mental health and more than ten years as a psychotherapist. These diverse populations include youth and adult offenders, communities impacted by Acquired Brain Injuries, refugees, war victims, and those needing crisis-based support in various settings, i.e., liaison with police, hospitals, community agencies, and inpatient mental health settings.

Harrison specializes in evidence-based therapies, including Cognitive Behavioural Therapy (CBT), Cognitive Processing Therapy (CPT), Dialectical Behavioural Therapy (DBT), Thought Developmental Practice (TDP), Acceptance and Commitment Therapy (ACT), Interpersonal therapy (IPT), Motivational Interviewing Techniques, Grounding Techniques, Integrative Eclectic Therapy, Humanistic Experiential Therapy, Interpersonal Therapy, Supportive Therapy, Exposure Therapy, Visual Therapy, Psychodynamic Therapy

# FOREWORD

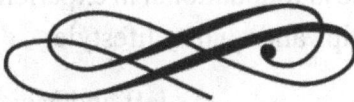

D r. Harrison Mungal's book "Valuing Your Value and Worth" is a book that is very relevant today. Many struggles with self-image, identity and resilience to move beyond their past.

We must fundamentally understand our worth and value to have an authentic self. Dr. Harrison provides research and professional expertise to help us discover our true selves and unlock our potential.

Many factors can contribute to a lack of self-worth and self-value. Specifically, this book will teach you that your past does not determine your future, successes or "who" you are. You will have access to tools to learn how to become resilient and have a new self-image and identity.

This book is a helpful resource that provides practical strategies to discover and reinforce your value. Some examples of valuable insights include combatting negative conditioning, celebrating successes, validating experiences, engaging in self-compassion and self-care, positive self-talk, and viewing setbacks as practical learning experiences.

This book is a must for anyone interested in improving their identity. A solid understanding of your worth and value is foundational in experiencing a healthy self, relationships and quality lifestyle.

Jeff and Maj-Britt Edwards

# TABLE OF CONTENT

ABOUT THE AUTHOR.................................................3

FOREWORD................................................................7

INTRODUCTION......................................................11

FEELING LIKE A FAILURE....................................15

CELEBRATING ACCOMPLISHMENTS.................29

THE POWER OF EMPATHY....................................37

HURT, ABUSED, AND TRAMATIZED...................49

OUR IDENTITY........................................................63

IDENTITY REDEFINED..........................................71

POSITIVE SELF – IMAGE........................................79

REBUILDING SELF-TRUST ....................................91

KINTSUGI .............................................................101

SELF-DISCOVERY.............................................109

HEIRLOOM ..........................................................117

CONCLUSION .....................................................127

# INTRODUCTION

*Valuing* **Your Value & Worth** is a book that focuses on clarifying who we are – and allowing that to spill over into every area of our lives. A clear understanding of value and worth is foundational in setting our relationship with ourselves and others. The key to such flourishing thoughts is getting the relationship with ourselves right and understanding the value and worth we carry.

Emotional wounds, including abuses, traumas, regrets, mistakes, wrongdoing, wrong choices, and weaknesses, can create emotional scars that can cheat us from seeing a bright future. We may develop beliefs that we are devalued and worthless. However, this book will change your mindset. You will learn how to move ahead regardless of your past.

Our past does not determine our success or define the "who" we are. Our choice of using the obstacles from the past as opportunities will keep us on track with our destiny. We can use the past to fertilize our future.

This book will teach you how to see the light at the end of the tunnel. How to have hope when you feel hopeless. How to become resilient and tap into the power of your mind. It will teach you how to affect others with a positive mindset.

You will learn about having a new identity as a champion over your past, a new self-image, understating the concept of Kintsugi, the principles of an heirloom, and more.

This is an exciting book as it teaches us to live with a new set of eyes and why we need to appreciate the "who" we are and not the "who" we were. You will learn why it is necessary to appreciate yourself and the power of forgiveness.

This is one of my best books written. The wealth of knowledge has been accumulated with time from past experiences of individuals struggling with self-worth and self-value. It gives insight into being transformed into a person you yourself will love. It will show you how valuable you are, and nothing can take that away.

You will learn to love yourself and not feel guilty about it.

Author: Harrison Mungal.

# FEELING *Like a* FAILURE

In the depths of our hearts, we all yearn to recognize and embrace our value and worth. Yet, there are moments in life when we find ourselves grappling with feelings of failure and inadequacy. During these challenging times, it becomes crucial to embark on a journey of self-discovery that allows us to see the inherent value within ourselves and others.

Our lives should serve as a guiding light, illuminating the path toward reclaiming our self-worth and fostering a positive outlook. We must acknowledge the intrinsic value and celebrate the worth in our lives and those around us.

Each of us possesses a unique essence, an inherent worth not contingent on external achievements or societal standards. We will uncover the truth that lies within, understanding that our worth is an irrevocable part of our being.

We need to unravel the layers of negative conditioning that have clouded our perception of self-worth. Society, upbringing, and past experiences can create a distorted lens through which we view ourselves. By untangling these threads, we can free ourselves from the shackles of self-doubt and unlock the full potential of our value.

In our journey of self-discovery, we can encounter self-doubt as a formidable adversary. However, armed with empowering techniques, we can learn to combat these thoughts and foster self-belief. We can build confidence and resilience to withstand self-doubt through practical strategies and empowering mindset shifts.

Embracing imperfections becomes a vital stepping stone on our path toward self-worth. We can learn to see beauty within our flaws in a world that often glorifies perfection. We can profoundly understand their contribution to our unique worth by embracing our imperfections. They remind us of our humanity and as catalysts for growth and personal development.

We must learn to celebrate our accomplishments, big and small, as beacons of our progress. Acknowledging these milestones reinforces our sense of worth and cultivates a positive self-perception. Through a lens of gratitude, we can recognize our achievements as stepping stones on the path to self-actualization.

Cultivating self-compassion becomes an essential practice on our transformative journey. We can learn to extend the same kindness and understanding to ourselves that we offer to others. We nurture a positive self-perception through self-compassion and cultivate an unwavering belief in our worth.

An essential aspect of recognizing worth lies in acknowledging the value in others. By embracing empathy and understanding, we develop a profound compassion toward the experiences of those around us. In recognizing the intrinsic worth of others, we forge connections that affirm our value and uplift the collective spirit.

Building positive relationships becomes a cornerstone of our journey. By nurturing connections rooted in respect, love, and support, we surround ourselves with individuals who affirm our worth and uplift us in times of doubt. Together, we create a community where the flame of self-worth burns brightly for all.

We can shift our perspectives on failure in our quest to reclaim our value and worth. Rather than seeing it as a mark of inadequacy, we can view failure as an opportunity for growth and self-discovery. We forge a path toward resilience and personal transformation by embracing the lessons hidden within our setbacks.

We must understand that cultivating gratitude and appreciation is a powerful tool. We find solace in the present moment through gratitude, recognizing the abundance surrounding us. By cultivating gratitude for ourselves and others, we foster a positive mindset that enhances our self-worth and enriches our lives.

As we embark on this transformative journey, let us embrace the power within us to recognize our value and worth. With each step we take, we can shed the heavy cloak of self-doubt and embrace the radiant light within us. Together, we will unveil the essence of our being, celebrating the remarkable worth within ourselves and others.

In a world that often measures our worth based on external achievements or superficial attributes, it is essential to recognize and embrace the concept of intrinsic value. Every one of us possesses an inherent worth simply by virtue of being human. Our value extends far beyond our accomplishments, appearance, or societal labels. It resides deep within us, waiting to be acknowledged and celebrated.

A spark of light exists at the core of our being, a unique essence that makes us who we are. This essence, this intrinsic value, is not determined by the opinions of others or the standards set by society. It is an inherent birthright, a fundamental truth that remains unwavering despite our challenges and setbacks.

Embracing our value and worth requires us to recognize and accept ourselves exactly as we are. It is about understanding that we are enough, worthy of love, respect, and happiness. We must release the need for external validation and learn to validate ourselves from within. This process begins with self-acceptance.

Self-acceptance is a powerful act of self-love. It involves embracing our unique qualities, quirks, and imperfections. Instead of striving for an idealized version of ourselves, we acknowledge and appreciate the beauty of our individuality. Accepting ourselves wholeheartedly, we tap into our true potential and unlock our limitless possibilities.

As we embark on recognizing our intrinsic value, it is essential to celebrate the qualities that make us who we are. Each of us possesses a tapestry of strengths, talents, and virtues that contribute to the richness of our lives. Some of us may have a gift for creativity, while others excel in analytical thinking. Some may possess a compassionate heart, while others inspire with leadership skills. These unique qualities are the building blocks of our intrinsic value, and by acknowledging and nurturing them, we enhance our self-worth.

Furthermore, our experiences, both triumphs and struggles, shape our intrinsic value. The challenges we have overcome, the lessons we have learned, and the resilience we have developed are testaments to our strength and worth. In these moments of growth and self-discovery, our intrinsic value shines brightest. We can transform our hardships into wisdom, embrace our vulnerabilities, and emerge stronger than before.

In recognizing our value and worth, we also understand that we are interconnected. Each person's worth is equally valuable, deserving of recognition and respect. By embracing our inherent value, we cultivate a deep sense of empathy and appreciation for the worth of others. We recognize that every individual has a unique journey and intrinsic value to contribute to the tapestry of humanity.

As we continue exploring and understanding our value and worth, let us do so with positivity and self-empowerment. Each step we take towards recognizing our worth is a step towards a more fulfilling and authentic life. By embracing our unique qualities, practicing self-acceptance, and celebrating our experiences, we amplify our intrinsic value and radiate it outwards, inspiring others to do the same.

Recognizing our value and worth is a transformative journey of self-discovery. We understand that our worth extends beyond external measures and societal expectations. We possess an inherent worth simply by being human, and by embracing our unique qualities and experiences, we unlock our limitless potential. Self-acceptance becomes a powerful self-love, empowering us to embrace our individuality and live authentically. As we recognize our value, we also recognize the value in others, fostering empathy and appreciation for the diverse tapestry of humanity.

Understanding value and worth helps to unravel the intricate web of negative conditioning that often leaves us questioning our inherent worthiness. We must explore the factors contributing to doubts and examine the societal influences, comparisons, and unrealistic expectations that can cloud our perception. Moreover, we must understand that we can provide empowering techniques to challenge and overcome negative conditioning, paving the way for a more positive and authentic self-perception.

In the hustle and bustle of our daily lives, it is all too easy to be influenced by external factors that undermine our sense of value. With its stringent standards and expectations, society can create a pervasive culture of comparison and self-doubt. We are bombarded with images and narratives that depict an idealized version of success, beauty, and happiness, leaving us feeling inadequate and unworthy. Recognizing that these societal influences do not define our worth is essential. They are constructs that often fail to capture each individual's depth and uniqueness.

Comparison, another insidious aspect of negative conditioning, can lead to self-deprecation and dissatisfaction. When we constantly measure ourselves against others, we overlook our strengths, accomplishments, and personal journey. We must remember that comparison is a thief of joy, robbing us of the ability to appreciate our unique qualities and contributions. We can break free from the detrimental comparison cycle by redirecting our focus inward and celebrating our progress and growth.

Unrealistic expectations, imposed by external sources and self-imposed, can also contribute to our negative conditioning. We may set impossibly high standards for ourselves, believing perfection is the only measure of worthiness. However, it is essential to recognize that perfection is an unattainable ideal. Embracing the beauty of imperfections and understanding that our worth is not contingent upon flawlessness allows us to release the burden of unrealistic expectations and embrace our authentic selves.

To challenge and overcome negative conditioning, we must first cultivate self-awareness. By examining our thoughts, beliefs, and patterns of self-judgment, we gain insight into the root causes of our self-doubt. This awareness empowers us to challenge and reframe the negative narratives that have become ingrained in our minds.

One powerful technique to combat negative conditioning is the practice of self-affirmations. We rewrite the narratives that diminish our self-worth by consciously and consistently affirming our inherent worth, strengths, and positive qualities. Affirmations act as gentle reminders of our unique values and help to counteract the negative conditioning that may have seeped into our subconscious.

Another empowering strategy is to surround ourselves with positive influences. We create a healthy ecosystem reinforcing our sense of worth by consciously curating our social environment and seeking supportive and uplifting relationships. Building a network of individuals who celebrate our successes, validate our experiences, and remind us of our value can be instrumental in overcoming negative conditioning.

Additionally, practicing self-compassion is vital in challenging and overcoming negative conditioning. Rather than berating ourselves for perceived failures or shortcomings, we must extend the same kindness and understanding we offer to others. Embracing self-compassion allows us to cultivate a nurturing internal dialogue that supports our self-worth and encourages growth and resilience.

As we navigate the path of unravelling negative conditioning, it is essential to remember that this process takes time and patience. It requires us to be gentle with ourselves to acknowledge that we are human and susceptible to the influence of external factors. By identifying the factors contributing to questioning our value, examining societal influences, comparisons, and unrealistic expectations, and employing empowering techniques to challenge and overcome negative conditioning, we take significant steps towards reclaiming our inherent worth and embracing our true selves. Through this transformative journey, we begin to recognize the immense value and worth that reside within us, independent of external validation or societal expectations.

In the intricate tapestry of our lives, self-doubt can cast a shadow over our perception of value and worth. It profoundly impacts how we see ourselves and our abilities, often leading us to underestimate our true potential. However, by acknowledging the power of self-doubt and embracing practical strategies to combat it, we can cultivate self-belief and unlock a world of limitless possibilities.

Self-doubt, like an invisible weight upon our shoulders, can colour our thoughts and cloud our judgment. It whispers words of inadequacy, planting seeds of uncertainty in our minds. It creates a barrier between us and our dreams, making us question whether we are truly capable or deserving of success. Yet, it is crucial to remember that self-doubt does not accurately reflect our abilities or worth. It is merely a product of our fears and insecurities stemming from a place of self-protection.

To overcome self-doubt, we must embark on self-discovery and self-empowerment. One practical strategy is to introduce affirmations into our daily lives. Affirmations are powerful statements we consciously repeat to ourselves, affirming our positive qualities and strengths. By consistently reinforcing positive self-beliefs, we create a fertile ground for self-confidence to flourish. Affirmations such as "I am capable," "I am deserving of success," and "I trust in my abilities" serve as gentle reminders of our worth and power.

Positive self-talk acts as a gentle guiding voice amidst the chaos of self-doubt. It involves consciously replacing negative thoughts with empowering and supportive words. Instead of dwelling on perceived shortcomings or failures, we focus on our achievements, progress, and unique qualities.

When faced with challenges, we remind ourselves of past victories and the resilience that lies within us. By nurturing a positive inner dialogue, we cultivate a mindset that believes in our abilities and reinforces our self-worth.

Reframing negative thoughts is another effective strategy to counter self-doubt. It involves consciously challenging and transforming negative interpretations of events or situations. Rather than viewing setbacks as failure indications, we see them as valuable learning experiences.

We can shift our perspective from "I can't do it" to "I haven't figured it out yet." This subtle shift in mindset empowers us to see challenges as opportunities for growth and development. It allows us to embrace the journey of learning and understand that setbacks are not a reflection of our worth but stepping stones toward success.

In our quest to overcome self-doubt, it is crucial to cultivate self-compassion. Self-compassion involves treating ourselves with kindness and understanding, especially in moments of doubt or perceived failure. We acknowledge that everyone faces challenges and makes mistakes, and we extend the same empathy and compassion to ourselves. By embracing self-compassion, we create a nurturing internal environment that encourages self-belief and resilience.

Additionally, seeking support from others can greatly assist us on this journey. Sharing our struggles and vulnerabilities with trusted individuals allows us to gain perspective and receive encouragement. Seeking guidance from mentors, coaches, or therapists can provide valuable insights and strategies to overcome self-doubt. Their support and expertise remind us that we are not alone in our struggles and that resources are available to help us on our path to self-belief.

We embark on a transformative journey as we implement these practical strategies and embrace the power of positive self-talk, affirmations, and reframing negative thoughts.

Self-doubt no longer holds us captive but becomes a catalyst for growth and self-discovery. We develop a profound sense of self-belief, recognizing that our worth extends far beyond the limitations we once imposed upon ourselves. With each step forward, we unlock our true potential and embrace a life with confidence and purpose.

We need to understand value and worth. Our value and what we are worth are priceless. Nothing we have done, what others have done to us, our weaknesses, mistakes, and wrongdoing can change the value and worth we carry.

# CELEBRATING ACCOMPLISHMENTS

As we continue our journey of discovering value and worth, one essential aspect we must explore is the power of celebrating accomplishments. These achievements profoundly impact our self-worth and well-being, whether significant milestones or tiny victories.

We need to recognize and acknowledge our accomplishments, embrace their positive effects on our self-perception, and provide guidance on setting realistic goals and measuring our progress.

There is immense value in taking the time to recognize and celebrate our achievements, no matter how big or small they may seem. Often, we are quick to downplay our successes, attributing them to luck or dismissing them as insignificant. However, by acknowledging and celebrating our accomplishments, we validate our efforts and honour our hard work in pursuing our goals.

When we celebrate our accomplishments, we send a powerful message to ourselves – that our efforts matter and we can achieve great things. This validation of our abilities and dedication boosts our self-confidence and self-worth. Each accomplishment serves as evidence of our capabilities, reminding us that we can overcome challenges and reach our desired outcomes.

Moreover, celebrating accomplishments fosters a positive mindset. Focusing on our achievements shifts our attention from self-doubt and negativity to a place of gratitude and positivity. This positive mindset becomes a catalyst for continued growth and self-belief. It fuels our motivation, inspires us to set new goals, and reinforces our belief in our potential.

To make the most of celebrating accomplishments, it is essential to set realistic goals that are meaningful and attainable. Setting unrealistic expectations can lead to frustration and feelings of failure. Instead, by setting goals within our reach, we set ourselves up for success and ensure that our accomplishments align with our abilities and aspirations.

When setting goals, it is beneficial to break them down into smaller, manageable tasks. This approach allows us to track our progress more effectively and celebrate milestones. By commemorating these incremental achievements, we maintain our momentum and stay motivated to continue working towards our larger goals.

Measuring progress is an essential part of goal-setting and celebrating accomplishments. We gain a sense of direction and purpose by establishing clear metrics or milestones. These measurable indicators provide tangible evidence of our progress and serve as checkpoints to assess how far we have come. It is important to remember that progress is not always linear. There may be setbacks and obstacles along the way, but it is through perseverance and resilience that we continue to move forward.

When measuring progress, we must focus on our growth and improvement rather than comparing ourselves to others. Each journey is unique, and what matters most is our personal development and the goals we have set for ourselves. By staying true to our path and acknowledging our progress, we cultivate a healthy and positive mindset that reinforces our sense of worth and accomplishment.

As we continue our journey of discovering value and worth, celebrating our accomplishments should be a culture we create. We should be at a pivotal section dedicated to cultivating self-compassion. Self-compassion, the gentle embrace of kindness and understanding towards oneself, plays a profound role in nurturing self-worth and fostering a positive self-perception. It allows us to create a nurturing internal environment that supports our growth and empowers us to overcome challenges with grace and resilience.

Exploring the concept of self-compassion unveils a wellspring of love and acceptance that resides within us. It involves recognizing that we are worthy of compassion and extending the same empathy and understanding to ourselves that we readily offer others. Self-compassion allows us to release the burden of self-judgment and self-criticism, replacing it with self-care and self-nurturing. This gives us all the reason to celebrate our accomplishments.

In our quest to cultivate self-compassion, it is essential to engage in practical exercises and techniques that enable us to embody this nurturing mindset. One such exercise is self-compassionate self-talk. When faced with difficulties or setbacks, we can consciously speak to ourselves with kindness and understanding. By reframing our inner dialogue and offering encouragement and support, we create a safe space within ourselves where self-worth can flourish.

Another concept to celebrate is the accomplishment of practicing self-forgiveness. We are all human and bound to make mistakes along our journey. Self-forgiveness allows us to acknowledge our imperfections and release ourselves from guilt and self-blame. By forgiving ourselves, we embrace our fallibility and recognize that mistakes do not define our worth.

Engaging in self-care and self-nurturing is integral to developing a positive self-perception. Taking time for activities that bring us joy, relaxation, and rejuvenation replenishes our spirit and reinforces the belief that we deserve love and care. Whether engaging in a hobby, spending time in nature, or indulging in self-care rituals, these acts of self-nurturing remind us of our inherent worth and cultivate a deeper connection with ourselves. This will bring a heart of celebration.

Practicing self-compassion involves acknowledging and honouring our emotions. It is essential to create space for our feelings, allowing ourselves to experience them fully without judgment. Whether sadness, anger, or frustration, each emotion is a valuable messenger, guiding us toward deeper self-awareness and understanding. By embracing our feelings with compassion, we learn to validate our own experiences and navigate life's challenges with greater resilience.

We must recognize that it is not a destination but a continuous practice to celebrate accomplishment. It requires patience, commitment, and gentle persistence. Just as a tender seedling requires nurturing to blossom into a vibrant flower, celebrating achievement requires our consistent attention and care.

Through self-compassion, we can develop a profound sense of self-acceptance and self-love, giving us another reason to celebrate. We learn to honour our strengths, acknowledge our efforts, and embrace our unique qualities. Rather than comparing ourselves to others or seeking external validation, we find solace in knowing that our worth is not dependent on others' opinions or societal standards.

As we embark on self-compassion, we are reminded of the importance of prioritizing self-care. Taking time for ourselves is not selfish; it is an act of self-preservation and self-honouring. When we nourish our spirit, body, and soul, we create a solid foundation from which our sense of worth can flourish.

Understanding the need to acknowledge areas in our lives to celebrate helps us understand our value and worth. Its

Empathy and understanding are among the most profound ways to connect with others and foster a sense of unity. When we extend ourselves to recognize and empathize with the experiences of others honestly, we not only acknowledge their inherent worth but also cultivate a more profound sense of compassion within ourselves. Again, more reasons to celebrate when we accomplish these goals in our lives.

# THE POWER *Of* EMPATHY

The transformative power of empathy highlights our value. And by building connections and promoting understanding among individuals from diverse backgrounds and walks of life, we can learn to see the value and worth in others.

Empathy is a guiding light that illuminates the path toward genuine connections and meaningful relationships. It allows us to step into another person's shoes, see the world through their eyes, and understand their joys, sorrows, and challenges. Doing so opens our hearts to a tapestry of human experiences, embracing the richness and diversity within our shared humanity.

When we approach others empathetically, we create a safe, nurturing space for open and honest communication. We demonstrate genuine care and concern for their well-being, showing them that their thoughts, feelings, and experiences matter. By actively listening and seeking to understand, we create an atmosphere of trust and vulnerability where individuals feel comfortable sharing their deepest thoughts and emotions.

Active listening plays a pivotal role in empathy and understanding. It involves hearing the spoken words and paying attention to the underlying emotions and unspoken messages. We profoundly respect the speaker's perspective when we listen attentively, without judgment or interruption. We demonstrate our commitment to understanding and valuing their experiences through active listening.

Open-mindedness is another essential aspect of empathy. It involves suspending our preconceived notions, biases, and judgments and approaching each interaction with a genuine willingness to learn and grow. Open-mindedness allows us to embrace diverse viewpoints and experiences, recognizing that each person's story is unique and valuable. We create space for mutual understanding and appreciation by letting go of rigid beliefs.

Empathy enables us to bridge the gaps between us, fostering connections that transcend differences in background, culture, or beliefs. It reminds us that we are all interconnected beneath the surface, sharing common hopes, dreams, and struggles. When we extend empathy towards others, we create a ripple effect of positivity and understanding that reverberates far beyond individual interactions.

By recognizing our value and worth, empathy becomes part of the culture we create in understanding others. It starts with small acts of kindness and compassion in our daily interactions – a gentle smile, a simple word of encouragement, or a comforting presence. These simple gestures can uplift others, affirm their worth, and instill a sense of belonging.

Empathy allows us to break down barriers and challenge stereotypes. By seeking to understand the experiences of those different from us, we foster an environment of acceptance and appreciation. We begin to see beyond the surface-level differences and recognize the shared human experiences that bind us.

In cultivating empathy, it is essential to remember that we all have unique stories and journeys. Each person's experiences shape their perception of the world and sense of self-worth. By listening and empathizing, we validate their experiences and demonstrate that their voices matter.

In recognizing our value and worth, the significance of surrounding ourselves with uplifting and supportive individuals cannot be overstated.

Positive relationships catalyze personal growth, affirming our worth and helping us thrive in all aspects of life. These relationships provide emotional support and create an environment where our inherent value is acknowledged and celebrated.

We need positive, empathetic relationships, and our empathy can be reciprocal. When we surround ourselves with positive influences, we create a nurturing and empowering ecosystem that uplifts our spirits and encourages us to reach for our dreams. These individuals believe in our potential, offering unwavering support and encouragement. Through their belief in us, they reinforce our self-belief and foster a deep sense of worthiness.

Building positive relationships starts with recognizing the qualities we seek in others and actively seeking out individuals who embody those qualities. Positivity, empathy, and authenticity are the pillars of these relationships. When we interact with others who radiate positivity, we are naturally drawn to their energy and find ourselves inspired to be the best version of ourselves.

A key aspect of building positive relationships is reciprocity - the mutual exchange of support and encouragement. Just as we seek uplifting individuals, we must strive to uplift others. By being a source of positivity, understanding, and encouragement, we create a nurturing environment where everyone's worth is recognized and celebrated. We experience a profound sense of connection and fulfillment through these reciprocal relationships.

Open and honest communication plays a pivotal role in building positive relationships. We create a safe space for vulnerability and genuine connection by actively listening to others and expressing ourselves authentically. Sharing our hopes, dreams, fears, and insecurities with trusted individuals deepens our bonds and reinforces our worth. In turn, we encourage others to share their experiences, strengthening the foundation of support and understanding.

Setting healthy boundaries is essential for maintaining positive relationships. We must recognize that our worth does not depend on the validation or approval of others. By establishing boundaries that protect our emotional well-being and respecting the boundaries of others, we cultivate relationships based on mutual respect and understanding. These boundaries ensure that our worth is upheld and that we engage in relationships that uplift and empower us.

In pursuing positive relationships that share empathy when needed, we must surround ourselves with individuals who inspire and challenge us to grow. This helps us to appreciate the value and worth we carry. These individuals can serve as mentors, guiding us toward our full potential and reminding us of our inherent worth. Through their wisdom and guidance, we gain valuable insights and better understand our capabilities.

Celebrating each other's successes is an integral part of building positive relationships. When we genuinely celebrate the appreciation of others, we reinforce their value and worth. We also demonstrate our belief in their abilities by encouragement to stay strong. By rejoicing in their victories, we cultivate an environment of support and encouragement, fostering a community where everyone's achievements are recognized and celebrated.

Exploring the transformative power of shifting our perspectives, particularly regarding failures and setbacks, is essential. Our minds can make us believe that our value and worth have been tinted or devalued. However, empathy will help us to regain ourselves and become resilient in sustaining ourselves.

It is essential to view our failures as opportunities for growth and personal development. By introducing techniques to reframe these challenges positively and emphasizing the value of self-reflection and learning, we can unlock new possibilities and deepen our understanding of our worth.

When faced with failure, it is natural to feel discouraged and disheartened. However, by examining these experiences through a different lens, we can uncover hidden opportunities for growth and self-discovery.

Viewing failures as stepping stones rather than roadblocks enables us to approach them with resilience and optimism. Instead of allowing failures to define us, we can harness their transformative power to propel us forward. This reduces the need for extreme empathy and becoming codependent on others.

One powerful technique for shifting our perspective is reframing. By reframing our failures, we actively choose to focus on the lessons learned and the growth potential rather than dwelling on the negative aspects. For instance, instead of perceiving a failed project as a personal shortcoming, we can view it as an opportunity to refine our skills, learn from our mistakes, and approach future endeavours with a more informed mindset. This shift in perspective empowers us to extract value from every setback, reinforcing our belief in our worth and potential.

Self-reflection plays a pivotal role in this process of shifting perspectives. Taking the time to introspect and analyze our failures' reasons allows us to understand ourselves and our actions better. Through self-reflection, we uncover valuable insights and identify areas for improvement. By embracing self-reflection as a powerful tool, we can transform failures into catalysts for personal growth and self-awareness.

Learning from past experiences is an invaluable aspect of shifting perspectives. Each failure carries a wealth of wisdom and knowledge that can inform our future endeavours. By identifying patterns and recognizing recurring challenges, we equip ourselves with the tools to navigate future obstacles more effectively. Learning from our mistakes and adapting our approach instills confidence in our abilities and reaffirms our worthiness of success.

Moreover, it is crucial to cultivate a growth mindset—a belief that our abilities and intelligence can be developed through dedication and effort. With a growth mindset, we embrace challenges as opportunities to stretch our capabilities and expand our potential. We recognize that failure is not a reflection of our worth but a natural part of learning. By nurturing a growth mindset, we foster resilience, curiosity, and an unwavering belief in our capacity to overcome setbacks and achieve our goals.

It is crucial to approach this journey of shifting perspectives with kindness and self-compassion. Reframing failures and setbacks, we must remember that mistakes are a typical human experience. Rather than berating ourselves for perceived shortcomings, we can extend grace and understanding. Self-compassion allows us to learn from our failures without internalizing them as reflections of our worth. It encourages us to treat ourselves with the same empathy and kindness we would offer to a dear friend, reinforcing a positive and supportive mindset.

As we navigate the intricate tapestry of life, one of the most powerful tools we have at our disposal for cultivating a positive mindset and recognizing our value and worth. Life's goal is never to lose sight of the priceless gem we are. Recognizing and acknowledging our value and worth creates a sense of independence, keeping us on track with our destiny.

Having gratitude is another form of not becoming codependent on empathy to sustain our value and worth. We need to explore the profound impact of appreciation and delve into various practices and techniques that can help us develop a grateful outlook toward ourselves and others. By embracing gratitude and expressing appreciation, we unlock a wealth of joy, contentment, and a deeper understanding of our worth.

Gratitude is a guiding light, illuminating the daily blessings and abundance surrounding us. It is an active recognition and appreciation of the positive aspects of our lives, both big and small. When we cultivate gratitude, we shift our focus from what is lacking to what is present, and in doing so, we foster a positive mindset that radiates warmth and contentment.

One way to embrace gratitude is by keeping a gratitude journal. This simple yet profound practice involves regularly writing down what we are grateful for.

It could be as simple as a beautiful sunrise, a kind word from a friend, or a moment of laughter shared with loved ones. By consciously acknowledging and documenting these moments of gratitude, we create a tangible reminder of the abundance in our lives, reinforcing our sense of worth and appreciation.

In moments of quiet reflection, we focus on the things we are grateful for, allowing a deep sense of gratitude to permeate our being. We can visualize the faces of loved ones, the opportunities we've been given, and the experiences that have shaped us. Through this practice, we cultivate a profound sense of appreciation and connection, nurturing our self-worth and recognizing the inherent value in our existence.

Expressing gratitude towards others is equally transformative. Taking the time to acknowledge and appreciate the people who have touched our lives in meaningful ways strengthens our relationships and reaffirms the value we see in them. Whether through heartfelt conversations, handwritten notes, or small acts of kindness, expressing our gratitude allows us to create a ripple effect of positivity and upliftment.

Furthermore, gratitude encourages us to recognize our strengths, achievements, and unique qualities. Too often, we downplay our worth and fail to acknowledge the incredible journeys we have embarked upon.

We fuel a positive self-image and nurture our worthiness by expressing gratitude for our growth, resilience, and inner strengths. This self-appreciation empowers us to embrace our authentic selves and radiate our unique light into the world.

In developing a grateful outlook, it is vital to cultivate a sense of mindfulness. Mindfulness allows us to fully immerse ourselves in the present moment, appreciating the beauty and blessings that exist here and now.

By grounding ourselves in the present, we open our hearts to the abundance surrounding us and deepen our connection with ourselves and others. It helps protect ourselves from falling into self-pity and making ourselves believe we have no value in life.

We must integrate gratitude into our daily routines and interactions to continuously create positive feedback. We must reinforce our sense of value and worth to stay strong and steady. Each day becomes a canvas for gratitude, a tapestry of appreciation that enriches our lives and nourishes our souls. This reduces the need for empathy, as much as it should be available with true friends and the relationships we develop. We need to avoid the codependent and move into the destiny God has for us.

# HURT, ABUSED, *and*
## TRAMATIZED

**H**ealing from emotional wounds is a profound and transformative journey that requires a deep understanding of their nature and impact on our lives. Unlike physical injuries that can be seen and treated, emotional wounds are often invisible, yet they carry significant weight within our psyche. These wounds can result from past traumas, abusive relationships, or other distressing experiences that have left lasting imprints on our thoughts, emotions, and overall well-being.

Hurt, abuse, and traumas create emotional wounds that affect our way of thinking. We tend to believe that we no longer carry the value and worth we should have. Some of us have devalued ourselves. However, our values and worth do not change because of past negative experiences. They don't determine who we are or our value and worth. God determines our value and worth and approves us, regardless of our past experiences.

Emotional wounds can take various forms, each with unique characteristics and effects. They can manifest as deep-seated pain that lingers within us, resurfacing during vulnerable moments. Fear may grip our hearts, making it difficult to trust others or engage fully in life. Anxiety may cloud our thoughts, leading to constant worry and a heightened sense of unease. Anger can simmer beneath the surface, arising from a sense of injustice or powerlessness. A profound sadness may permeate our being, casting a shadow over our daily experiences.

These emotional wounds shape our beliefs about ourselves and the world around us. When we have been hurt, betrayed, or violated, it can distort our perception of our value and the worth we carry. We may internalize negative messages and develop a critical inner voice that undermines our self-esteem. The wounds can influence our behaviours, leading us to engage in self-sabotaging patterns or seek out unhealthy relationships that mirror our past pain. Our ability to connect authentically with others may be hindered as we guard ourselves against the potential for further harm.

To embark on the healing path, it is crucial to understand the nature of these emotional wounds.

Acknowledging their existence and recognizing their impact is the first step toward recovery. By shining a light on these wounds, we can unravel their complex layers and gain insight into how they have influenced our lives.

Self-awareness is a powerful tool in this healing journey. It involves turning inward and cultivating a compassionate curiosity toward our thoughts, emotions, and reactions. Self-reflecting allows us to identify patterns, triggers, and behaviours rooted in our past wounds. This awareness enables us to make conscious choices and responses rather than being driven by unconscious ways that no longer serve us.

Furthermore, understanding that emotional wounds do not define us is crucial. They are part of our story but do not have to dictate our present or future. Recognizing that healing is possible and that we can reclaim our lives is an empowering realization. It allows us to shift our perspective from victimhood to resilience and take ownership of our healing process.

Healing emotional wounds is not a linear or quick process. It requires a commitment to self-care and self-compassion. It involves engaging in practices that nourish our soul (mind, will and emotions), body, and spirit. This may include therapy, meditation, journaling, engaging in creative outlets, seeking support from trusted individuals, and practicing healthy boundaries.

By actively tending to our emotional well-being and honouring our needs, we create a solid foundation for healing.

As we venture into the realm of healing from emotional wounds, it becomes imperative to grasp the profound and lasting effects such injuries can have on our self-esteem and sense of worth. We could feel devalued.

Emotional wounds stemming from hurt, abuse, or trauma can permeate deep into the core of our being, leaving scars that may not be visible to the naked eye but are felt intensely within our hearts and minds.

When we experience emotional wounds, our self-esteem often takes a considerable blow. We may begin to doubt our worthiness, questioning whether we deserve love, respect, and happiness. Negative beliefs about ourselves can take root, whispering destructive messages undermining our confidence and sense of value. These wounds may also create a distorted lens through which we view ourselves, causing us to perceive ourselves as broken, damaged, or unworthy of care and compassion.

Moreover, emotional wounds have a profound impact on our sense of worth. They can leave us feeling devalued, as if we do not deserve life's goodness. We may internalize the hurtful words or actions directed at us, believing we are inherently flawed or unlovable. The weight of these wounds can be burdensome, casting a shadow on our self-perception and inhibiting our ability to recognize and embrace our true worth.

To embark on the healing journey, it is crucial to acknowledge and process the emotions associated with our trauma. It can be tempting to bury these emotions deep within ourselves, hoping to move on and forget. However, true healing requires us to face our pain head-on, sit with our feelings, and allow ourselves to experience the full range of our emotions.

Acknowledging our emotions creates a safe space to express our pain, anger, sadness, or confusion. It allows us to validate our experiences and honour our emotions' depth. By permitting ourselves to feel, we acknowledge the significance of our emotional wounds and open the door to healing.

Healing, however, is not a linear or finite process. It is a journey that unfolds over time, requiring patience, compassion, and self-reflection. It is an ongoing and multifaceted process encompassing various aspects of our being—physical, emotional, mental, and spiritual.

Healing involves tending to our emotional wounds with tenderness and care. It entails seeking professional help, such as therapy or counselling, where we can explore our trauma in a safe and supportive environment. Through treatment, we can gain insight into the origins and impact of our emotional wounds, learn coping mechanisms, and develop strategies for self-care.

Additionally, healing requires self-compassion as we learn to treat ourselves with kindness and understanding. We must practice self-care and nurture ourselves in ways that replenish our emotional well-being. This can involve engaging in activities that bring us joy, connecting with supportive friends or family, or engaging in creative outlets that allow us to express ourselves authentically.

As we journey through the healing process, we must remember that healing is not a destination but a continuous evolution. It is a process of growth, self-discovery, and self-empowerment. Along the way, we may experience setbacks and challenges, but with each step forward, we cultivate resilience and strengthen our capacity to heal.

Holding onto hope and believing in our inherent worth is crucial in the face of emotional wounds. We can heal, reclaim our self-esteem, and recognize the immeasurable value that resides within us. By embracing the ongoing and multifaceted nature of healing, we can navigate the path toward emotional well-being, rediscover our sense of worth, and ultimately embark on a journey of self-restoration.

Healing emotional wounds requires a deliberate and compassionate approach as we strive to create a safe and supportive environment that nurtures our healing journey. Establishing such an environment begins with acknowledging the importance of our emotional well-being and prioritizing it in our lives. We can surround ourselves with people who understand and validate our experiences, individuals who provide a listening ear without judgment or expectation. Their presence alone can offer a sense of solace and support, reminding us that we are not alone in our healing process.

Within this safe space, self-reflection becomes a powerful tool for healing. By allowing ourselves to delve into our thoughts, emotions, and memories, we open the door to understanding the impact of our past experiences on our present state. Self-reflection offers an opportunity for introspection, where we can explore the depths of our emotions and thoughts, gaining insights into the wounds that still linger within us. Through this process, we can gradually unravel the layers of pain and begin to make peace with our past.

As we embark on our healing journey, self-compassion becomes essential to our approach. It involves treating ourselves with kindness, understanding, and empathy. We learn to embrace our vulnerabilities and acknowledge the pain we have endured. Rather than criticizing ourselves for our perceived weaknesses or shortcomings, we extend love and acceptance to every part of our being. Self-compassion becomes a guiding light, gently reminding us that we are worthy of healing and deserving of the care and understanding we offer ourselves.

Engaging in therapeutic approaches tailored to our needs can significantly support healing emotional wounds. Trauma-focused therapy offers a specialized technique to process and integrate traumatic experiences, helping us regain control and security. Cognitive-behavioural treatment enables us to identify and challenge negative thought patterns and beliefs, replacing them with healthier and more empowering ones. Expressive arts therapy provides a creative outlet for exploring emotions and expressing ourselves, allowing for healing through various artistic mediums such as painting, writing, or music. These therapeutic approaches can be instrumental in uncovering deep-rooted wounds, promoting healing, and fostering personal growth.

In addition to therapeutic interventions, incorporating mindfulness and relaxation techniques into our daily lives can significantly support our emotional well-being. Mindfulness invites us to be fully present at the moment, observing our thoughts and emotions without judgment. By practicing mindfulness, we develop a deeper understanding of ourselves and our inner experiences. It allows us to cultivate a sense of calm and centeredness, creating space for healing and self-compassion.

Relaxation techniques, such as deep breathing exercises, progressive muscle relaxation, or meditation, help to soothe our nervous system, reduce stress, and promote emotional balance. These practices can be integrated into our routines, providing us with moments of respite and nurturing our emotional well-being.

The strategies for healing emotional wounds require establishing a safe and supportive environment, fostering self-reflection and self-compassion, engaging in therapeutic approaches tailored to our needs, and incorporating mindfulness and relaxation techniques into our lives. With patience, self-care, and the support of others, we can embark on a transformative journey of healing, gradually finding solace, self-acceptance, and emotional well-being.

Within this healing space, we can rediscover our worth and value, embracing the fullness of our being and reclaiming our power to create a life filled with joy, resilience, and meaning.

Personal power is the inner resiliency, strength and agency of each individual. It is the ability to assert oneself, make choices, and take action in alignment with one's values and goals. In the context of the recovery process, personal power plays a crucial role in rebuilding one's life after trauma. However, it is essential to acknowledge that trauma can significantly impact an individual's perception of personal power.

Trauma can potentially shatter a person's sense of control and autonomy. It can leave individuals feeling helpless, powerless, and stripped of their agency. The experiences of hurt, abuse, and trauma can create a deep-seated belief that they are fundamentally flawed or unworthy of asserting themselves and making choices. These disempowering beliefs can further perpetuate a cycle of victimhood and hinder the healing process.

Reclaiming personal power involves challenging these disempowering beliefs and recognizing that trauma does not define one's worth or capabilities. It requires a shift in perspective, acknowledging that the trauma was an external event that happened to them but does not have to define their identity or future. It involves taking responsibility for one's healing journey and reclaiming the power to make choices that lead to personal growth and well-being.

In the aftermath of trauma, it is common for individuals to underestimate their resilience and strength. However, it is essential to acknowledge that resilience is an innate quality within each individual. It is the ability to bounce back from adversity, adapt to challenging circumstances, and thrive in adversity.

Exploring the innate resilience within individuals who have experienced trauma involves recognizing the courage and strength they have demonstrated throughout their lives. It means acknowledging the countless times they have faced adversity and found ways to persevere. By reflecting on past experiences, individuals can understand their inherent resilience and draw inspiration from their triumphs over difficult situations.

Identifying personal strengths is another crucial aspect of rediscovering personal power and resilience. Each person possesses unique strengths: resilience, compassion, creativity, and determination. These strengths can serve as sources of empowerment, reminding individuals of their capabilities and that they have the inner resources to overcome their challenges.

Cultivating resilience involves engaging in self-reflection and acknowledging personal growth. It means recognizing and celebrating the progress made along the healing journey, no matter how small. Positive affirmations can be powerful tools in reinforcing a resilient mindset, reminding individuals of their strengths and abilities. Embracing challenges with a growth mindset, and viewing them as opportunities for learning and growth, can further cultivate resilience.

By understanding personal power, recognizing the influence of trauma, challenging disempowering beliefs, exploring resilience, identifying unique strengths, and cultivating resilience through self-reflection, positive affirmations, and embracing challenges, individuals can rediscover their strengths and reclaim their power. This process of self-empowerment and resilience-building is an essential part of the recovery journey after trauma, allowing individuals to move forward with confidence, purpose, and a renewed sense of worth.

Trauma profoundly impacts our sense of self and how we perceive ourselves. When we experience hurt, abuse, or trauma, it can significantly shape our self-perception and identity. The wounds inflicted upon us can lead to shame, guilt, and worthlessness, distorting our understanding of who we are at our core.

In the aftermath of trauma, individuals often face common challenges in their identity development. They may struggle with a diminished sense of self-worth and a loss of trust in themselves and others. The trauma can redefine their identity, casting them into the role of a victim or survivor, and this narrative can become deeply ingrained. It can be challenging to break free from this identity label and find a new sense of self that goes beyond the trauma.

We need to come to a place of understanding that healing emotional wounds from past hurts, abuse, and traumas is essential. We cannot allow negative thoughts to affect our thinking of "who" we are. We can quickly devalue ourselves and fall back into old patterns under stress. Our old habits and behaviours can soon take over our minds.

The need to keep a clear identity of our current present life is a necessity. We are thinking godly thoughts, reconditioning our minds with words of affirmation, and restructuring how we speak. We need to hear ourselves speak positive words. We must affirm the "who" we are, not the "who" we were.

# **OUR** IDENTITY

❧

Our identities are like intricate tapestries woven from myriad threads representing our experiences, beliefs, values, and relationships. They are not simple or one-dimensional; they are complex and ever-evolving. Our identities encompass various aspects of our lives, such as our cultural background, gender, sexuality, profession, and personal interests. Each thread contributes to the vibrant mosaic that makes us who we are.

Identity goes far beyond the superficial labels imposed by society. It delves into the depths of our being, revealing the unique combination of qualities and attributes that define us as individuals. Through this exploration, we understand the intricate layers that shape us. By recognizing and appreciating the complexities of our identity, we open ourselves up to a deeper understanding of ourselves and others.

It is crucial to look beyond these surface-level identifications in a world that often seeks to categorize and label us. Society tends to impose expectations and stereotypes based on gender, race, age, and social status. However, identity goes beyond these external markers.

Embracing the uniqueness of our identity means recognizing that we are more than the labels assigned to us. It involves understanding that everyone has a rich tapestry of experiences, perspectives, and aspirations. It requires us to challenge societal norms and expectations, freeing ourselves from the constraints that restrict our authentic expression.

We empower ourselves to define our own identity by going beyond surface labels. We embrace the freedom to be true to ourselves, unapologetically embracing our passions, interests, and beliefs. In doing so, we cultivate a sense of authenticity and empowerment that radiates from within, allowing us to live our lives in alignment with our true selves.

As we embark on this life journey, we can appreciate the beauty in "who" we are and the value and worth we carry. We need to identify our unique blend of experiences, cultures, and perspectives that gives us worth. This means we have a purpose of living for, not allowing our past mistakes, wrongdoing, weaknesses, flaws, and regrets to cheat us from life. As we grasp a hold of our identity, we will embrace reason for living with our heads up high, knowing no one can approve of us but ourselves.

Ultimately, exploring the essence of our identity goes beyond a mere intellectual exercise. It is a deeply personal and transformative journey that allows us to embrace fully and appreciate the intrinsic worth and value of who we are. By understanding the multifaceted nature of our identity and going beyond surface labels, we unlock the true potential and power within ourselves, living a life of authenticity and purpose.

In today's society, we are often labelled and judged based on gender, race, ethnicity, religion, sexual orientation, and many other factors. These labels can limit our potential and create personal growth and fulfillment barriers. However, we can defy these labels and embrace the uniqueness of the "who" we are, not the "who" we were.

Overcoming stereotypes is essential to breaking free from societal expectations and labels. Stereotypes are preconceived notions about groups of people that are often based on incomplete or inaccurate information. For example, women are often stereotyped as emotional and irrational, while men are seen as aggressive and dominant. These stereotypes can be damaging and limiting, and it is essential to challenge and overcome them.

Stereotyping can become an obstacle to healing our emotional wounds. They can be responsible for blinding us from seeing the actual value we have and the worth we carry. They can belittle to live in shame and guilt. We must see ourselves as champions and heroes to those around us, even if they don't recognize it. We need to champion our past so we can be heroes for tomorrow.

By challenging stereotypes, we can break free from the labels imposed on us and create a more authentic and fulfilling life. We can assert our individuality and define ourselves based on our values and experiences rather than conforming to societal expectations. Overcoming stereotypes requires us to be brave and take risks, but it is a step toward proper personal growth and self-actualization.

Celebrating uniqueness is another crucial step in defying labels and embracing our identities. Each of us has unique experiences, values, and perspectives. We can create a sense of empowerment and fulfillment by embracing our individuality. We can also learn to appreciate the diversity within our communities and recognize each person's value.

Embracing our uniqueness also means accepting and celebrating our victories from overcoming our past hurts, traumas, and emotional wounds. We can create a more supportive community that values the worth we carry.

In a world that often pressures us to conform and fit into predefined moulds, embracing authenticity becomes an act of courage and self-liberation. It is within the depths of our identity and understanding that our past does not determine who we are, that makes a difference in moving on. We can find a wellspring of power to rise above our circumstances and move towards a bright future. We can embrace our authentic selves and honour our unique qualities, passions, and perspectives.

By embracing ourselves, we unlock a sense of liberation and freedom. We no longer need to mould ourselves into someone we are not; instead, we can fully express our true essence. This authenticity radiates through our actions, choices, and interactions with the world.

Embracing ourselves is not always easy. It requires self-reflection, self-acceptance, and the courage to stand in our truth, even when it may be uncomfortable or met with resistance. However, the rewards are immense. When we embrace our authentic identity, we align ourselves with our core values and passions, creating a profound sense of fulfillment and purpose.

Moreover, we enhance our self-worth. We cultivate a deep sense of self-respect and self-love by accepting and valuing ourselves for who we are. We recognize that our worth is not determined by external validation or societal expectations but by the inherent value, we possess as unique individuals.

Within our identity of being champions over our past hurts lies a wellspring of untapped potential waiting to be unleashed. When we fully embrace and understand who we are, we tap into a source of power and inspiration that propels us forward. This potential is not limited to personal growth but extends to our ability to empower and inspire others.

As we embrace our identity for not giving up and recognize our strengths, we gain the confidence to pursue our dreams and aspirations. We set audacious goals, challenge ourselves to grow, and break through self-imposed limitations. This self-empowerment is contagious, inspiring others to do the same.

By sharing our authentic stories and experiences, we create a ripple effect of empowerment. We use our obstacles as opportunities to grow. When others witness our journey of self-discovery and growth, they will find the courage to explore and embrace their own hurts and emotional wounds. We become catalysts for change, encouraging others to step into their power, overcome obstacles, and pursue their passions.

Unleashing our potential also involves leveraging our unique perspectives and talents to contribute meaningfully to the world. Our identity gives us a different lens through which we view the world, enabling us to bring fresh ideas, innovation, and diverse viewpoints to various spheres of life. By sharing our insights and making our voices heard, we can shape conversations, challenge the status quo, and drive positive change.

We must be reminded that our identity holds immense potential for self-empowerment and the empowerment of others. By embracing ourselves as champions, we enhance our self-worth. We appreciate ourselves for not giving up, regardless of how deep the emotional wounds were. We celebrate our identity as a winner, an influencer, and a role model.

This identity catalyzes personal growth and inspires others to embark on transformative journeys—an encouragement to give up and never feel like a failure or a loser. Your life can be catapulted into the future with the strength derived from a winning identity. We can profoundly impact ourselves, our communities, and the world.

# **IDENTITY** REDEFINED

I t is essential to acknowledge that identity is fluid and has the potential for positive growth and change. Redefining our identity after trauma requires intentional and compassionate effort. Cultivating self-acceptance and self-compassion is a vital first step. It means embracing ourselves, scars and all, and recognizing that we are not defined solely by our past experiences. By extending kindness and understanding towards ourselves, we can begin to heal the wounds inflicted by trauma and foster a more positive self-image.

Exploring our values, goals, and aspirations becomes essential to the identity redefinition process. Reflecting on what truly matters to us, what brings us joy and fulfillment, allows us to reconnect with our authentic

...s. These core values and aspirations serve as ...ding principles as we navigate the journey of identity ...discovery. They help us align our actions and choices with our true selves, enabling us to build a more meaningful and fulfilling life.

To redefine our identity positively, seeking opportunities for personal growth and engaging in new interests and passions is crucial. Trauma may have limited our sense of possibility. Still, by actively pursuing activities that bring us joy and ignite our curiosity, we can expand our horizons and discover new facets of ourselves. Trying new hobbies, exploring creative outlets, or engaging in community initiatives can open doors to personal growth and transformation.

Throughout this process of redefining our identity, it's important to remember that it is not a linear journey. There will be ups and downs, moments of self-doubt, and setbacks. But with each step forward, we gain a deeper understanding of ourselves and our resilience. Through these moments of growth, we reclaim our power and reshape our identity, emerging more assertively and authentically aligned with who we are meant to be.

In the depths of pain and adversity, a transformative potential is waiting to be realized. Post-traumatic growth is a profound phenomenon that emerges from the ashes of trauma. When faced with unimaginable challenges, individuals can rise above their circumstances and find meaning and purpose in their experiences.

Post-traumatic growth begins with acknowledging the depth of the pain endured. It is not about denying or minimizing the trauma but recognizing its profound impact on one's life. By bravely facing the wounds, individuals open themselves up to the possibility of growth and transformation. They understand that pain does not have to define them; it can catalyze personal growth.

Individuals can uncover a newfound sense of purpose within the crucible of suffering. Through the journey of healing, they discover the strength and resilience within themselves. They recognize that their experiences can inspire and motivate others who have walked similar paths. By sharing their stories, they can provide solace, hope, and guidance to those still grappling with their wounds.

Reflection becomes an invaluable tool in the quest for personal growth and transformation. It is a moment of introspection where individuals delve deep within themselves to uncover their core values and passions. This process teaches them what truly matters and what stirs their soul.

Identifying areas of interest or causes that align with one's experiences is essential in discovering personal purpose. It is about finding that sweet spot where personal history intersects with the potential for positive impact. By drawing upon their struggles, individuals can empathize with others facing similar challenges and offer support, guidance, and understanding.

Taking steps towards engaging in meaningful activities or advocacy work is where purpose truly comes alive. It is the transformative act of translating intention into action. By aligning personal values with real-world initiatives, we can actively contribute to improving ourselves and our communities. Whether volunteering for a cause, participating in awareness campaigns, or creating support networks, every step taken is a testament to our resilience and commitment to making a difference. Our value and worth become evident as we boldly break the shame, guilt and intimidates that may try to cripple our minds.

By transforming pain into purpose, we find healing for ourselves and become beacons of hope for others. Our journey becomes a source of inspiration and empowerment, reminding us of the human capacity to rise above adversity.

By embracing our past experiences, we unlock a powerful force that propels us toward personal growth, creating a brighter, more compassionate world.

Forgiveness has a profound transformative power, liberating us from hurt, abuse, and trauma. It is an intricate process, rather than a singular event, that allows us to reclaim our inner peace and move towards healing and growth. By exploring the benefits of forgiveness, we can unlock a path toward personal liberation and inner freedom. This brings light to the value and worth we carry.

Forgiveness, first and foremost, is an act of self-compassion. When we choose to forgive, we extend understanding and empathy toward ourselves. It is essential to recognize that forgiveness does not condone or excuse the harmful behaviour inflicted upon us. Instead, it serves as a tool to release the burden of resentment and anger that weighs heavily on our hearts.

Understanding forgiveness requires acknowledging the depth of pain and trauma endured. It is not an immediate or linear journey but rather a gradual unfolding of healing and acceptance. It involves confronting and acknowledging the emotions associated with the hurt, abuse, or trauma, allowing ourselves the space and time to process these feelings with compassion and care.

Moreover, forgiveness does not absolve the abuser or perpetrator of their actions. It is not about granting them a free pass or diminishing the gravity of their wrongdoing. Instead, forgiveness empowers survivors to regain control over their narrative and reclaim their power. It is a courageous act of choosing not to let the past define or dictate one's future.

Holding onto resentment and anger can profoundly impact our emotional well-being and hinder our journey toward healing. Though understandable given the circumstances, these emotions often keep us anchored in the past, preventing us from embracing the present and moving toward a brighter future. We can begin letting go by practicing forgiveness, self-compassion, and understanding.

Examining the impact of resentment and anger allows us to understand how they perpetuate our suffering. These emotions breed negativity and consume our energy, leaving little room for healing and personal growth. They can create a cycle of bitterness that traps us in perpetual victimhood, hindering our ability to rebuild and thrive.

Practicing forgiveness begins with extending compassion towards ourselves. It involves acknowledging the pain we have endured, validating our emotions, and allowing ourselves to grieve. We permit ourselves to heal through self-compassion, recognizing that we deserve peace and happiness.

Forgiveness rituals or therapeutic techniques can serve as powerful tools in the journey of letting go. These practices may vary from person to person, but they often involve intentional acts to release the emotional burden. Engaging in forgiveness rituals, such as writing letters to ourselves or the abuser (which may or may not be sent), performing symbolic acts of letting go, or seeking guidance from a therapist, can facilitate the process of forgiveness and aid in releasing resentment and anger.

In the realm of therapy, various therapeutic modalities, such as cognitive-behavioural therapy (CBT), acceptance and commitment therapy (ACT), or eye movement desensitization and reprocessing (EMDR), can provide valuable support in navigating the path of forgiveness and letting go. These approaches offer techniques to reframe our thoughts, process emotions, and develop coping strategies, ultimately fostering healing and facilitating the release of negative emotions.

Bringing healing to our emotional wounds is essential. Redefining our identity will bring us closer to accepting the priceless life we have. This is the starting point of freeing our soul from our past hurts can cripple thoughts from receiving the value and worth we carry. When we lose ourselves to thinking we are worthless because of our past mistakes, faults, and regrets, we devalue the "who" we are. We must rebuild ourselves to accept that we cannot change the past but our future. And the past does not determine who we are. It's the decision we make to move ahead with ourselves.

We need to accept our new identity as a refugee from another, like a permanent resident card or citizenship of a new country. We leave the old behind and welcome the new. The benefits that come with the new. The new embraces us and allows the latest to give even more value and worth for not giving up on ourselves. We rebuild ourselves; we rebuild self-trust. We can now trust ourselves to make wiser decisions and prevent any more emotional wounds.

# POSITIVE SELF – IMAGE

In the quest for a positive self-image, it is crucial to acknowledge that our identity holds inherent worth. We are not defined solely by external factors or achievements but by the essence of our being. Understanding this intrinsic value allows us to move beyond superficial judgments and embrace the richness of our authentic selves.

Nurturing our value and worth is fundamental to cultivating a positive self-image. It involves acknowledging and appreciating our unique qualities without comparing ourselves to others. This process requires self-compassion and a shift in focus from perceived flaws to our strengths and accomplishments. By embracing our individuality, we can build a foundation of self-worth that withstands external judgments and societal pressures.

Developing a positive self-image is an ongoing journey that requires active self-reflection and intentional practices. It involves cultivating self-awareness and challenging negative self-perceptions that may have been ingrained over time. By consciously recognizing our worth, we can break free from the limitations imposed by self-doubt and insecurities.

One powerful approach to nurturing value and worth is practicing gratitude. Taking time to appreciate the qualities, skills, and experiences contributing to our identity fosters a sense of fulfillment and self-validation. Gratitude shifts our focus to the positive aspects of our lives and reminds us of the unique contributions we bring to the world.

Another essential aspect of developing a positive self-image is surrounding ourselves with positive people. Connecting with others who appreciate and celebrate our value and worth creates a nurturing environment for personal growth and self-acceptance. By fostering relationships based on authenticity and mutual respect, we can build a network of encouragement that reinforces our self-worth.

Cultivating a positive self-image is a transformative process requiring patience, self-love, and resilience. It is about embracing the full spectrum of our identity, recognizing our inherent value, and nurturing self-acceptance. As we embark on this journey, we empower ourselves to live authentically and radiate confidence from within, positively impacting our relationships, aspirations, and overall well-being.

By embracing our authentic selves, we can forge genuine connections with others. When we allow ourselves to be vulnerable and share our true thoughts, beliefs, and values, we create an environment of honesty and openness. By shedding the masks, we wear to fit in; we invite others to do the same, fostering a space where authentic connections can flourish.

Embracing our value and worth enables us to attract like-minded individuals who appreciate us for who we indeed are. When we are genuine and authentic, we emit a sense of confidence and self-assuredness that resonates with others. We no longer seek validation or acceptance by pretending to be someone we're not. Instead, we attract connections that value and appreciate our true selves, forming relationships built on a foundation of understanding and authenticity.

Meaningful relationships are nurtured through authenticity, trust, and shared values. When we embrace our self-image, the value and worth we carry, we create a solid foundation for building healthy relationships.

Self-image and how we think of ourselves allow room to show what honesty looks like, letting others know and understand us on a deeper level. We create a space where trust can thrive by sharing our vulnerabilities, hopes, and dreams.

Trust is the cornerstone of any meaningful relationship. When we are authentic, we demonstrate our willingness to be transparent and genuine, fostering an environment where trust can be built and nurtured.

As we establish trust with ourselves and others, we create a safe space to feel comfortable expressing our true thoughts and emotions without fear of judgment or rejection. These deep connections based on trust allow for honest and open communication, leading to more robust, more fulfilling relationships.

Shared values also play a crucial role in building meaningful connections. When we can appreciate ourselves for the value we see in ourselves and our worth, social anxiety will not play a role in our lives. When we can align ourselves with our values, we naturally gravitate toward individuals who share similar beliefs and principles. These values form the basis for shared experiences, mutual support, and a sense of belonging. Building relationships with individuals who align with our values strengthens our connections and provides a sense of community and support.

Every individual possesses unique gifting and talents. Our value and worth are how we see ourselves and others. It combines our background, experiences, skills, knowledge, education, beliefs, and values. Through self-expression, we can truly convey who we are to the world. When we tap into the power of who we are, we discover a profound means of communication beyond words. Our voice reflects our true self, resonating with wisdom and strength.

By leveraging our self-image, we can express our passions, talents, and perspectives. Whether through art, music, writing, or public speaking, we can share our thoughts and emotions in ways that resonate deeply with others. Our voice becomes a powerful tool for connection and understanding, as it invites others to glimpse into our world and fosters empathy and compassion.

Moreover, using our voice is not just about personal expression; it also holds the potential to create positive change in the world around us. When we align our voices with the value and worth we see in ourselves, we can advocate for causes that matter to us, promote social justice, and inspire others to take action. Through our authentic self-expression, we can become catalysts for meaningful transformation.

When we recognize the power of self-expression, we also realize its potential to empower others. By sharing our stories, challenges, and triumphs, we encourage those around us to embrace their unique self-image and find the courage to express themselves authentically. We become beacons of inspiration, shining a light on the path of self-discovery and self-acceptance.

Moreover, having the freedom to express our healing from emotional wounds can be a potent force for supporting others. Through our words and actions, we can dismantle barriers, promote understanding, and inspire others to pursue a better future. We can tap into the value and worth we carry to make a difference in our lives and those around us.

In this journey of creating change in how we see ourselves, it is essential to embrace who we are. We must appreciate who we are regardless of age, sex, marital status, skin colour, height, weight, culture and ethnicity. We need to foster a culture of inclusivity and collaboration with ourselves.

The power of understanding ourselves and our self-image cannot be underestimated. By leveraging our self-image, we can appreciate the value and worth we carry. We can tap into a wellspring of personal fulfillment and forge connections with others. Through our voice, we not only communicate our truth but also have the potential to create positive change and empower others to see their value and worth.

In a world where individuals come from various backgrounds, cultures, and experiences, it is crucial to recognize the inherent value and significance that diversity brings to our lives. Valuing differences means acknowledging each person's unique perspectives, talents, and contributions. It involves embracing the richness that stems from diverse identities, such as race, ethnicity, gender, sexual orientation, religion, and socioeconomic background.

By appreciating who we are regardless of our past hurts, abuse, traumas and emotional wounds, we can open ourselves up to new ideas, ways of thinking, and ways of living. We can live life to its fullest like tomorrow does not exist, treating each person with dignity and respect.

Our value and worth will not allow our insecurities to pop its head up or our confidence level to drop. Our victories will allow us to break free from narrow-mindedness and expand our horizons to see the value and worth in others. We can develop the ability to mentor and guide others who may have been in the same state of mind of defeat.

Mentors play a vital role in helping others to navigate the complexities of their hurts and to see the light at the end of the tunnel. Mentors provide valuable insight, wisdom, and emotional support as individuals grapple with self-discovery questions and their value and worth.

A mentor's role goes beyond offering advice; they actively listen, empathize, and encourage others to explore their healing for their emotional wounds. By sharing their experiences and challenges, mentors help individuals realize they are not alone. They can bring light to how self-image is affected by emotional wounds, which play a significant role in how a person sees the value they carry.

Through mentorship, others can gain valuable perspectives, receive constructive feedback, and learn effective strategies for personal growth. Mentors can help others develop self-awareness, create a positive identity and self-image, and embrace the past to fertilize the future.

Mentors inspire and empower others to live authentically, allowing them to shape their lives confidently and purposefully.

Change is an inevitable part of life; within it lies the immense potential for personal growth and transformation. Embracing change means acknowledging that our past does not determine our future. It does not change our value and worth but fuels an evolving entity. It requires a willingness to step out of our comfort zones and explore new possibilities. By embracing change, we open ourselves to new experiences, challenges, and opportunities that can shape us into the best versions of ourselves.

When we embrace change, we embark on a journey of self-discovery. We spend more time future-oriented than allowing our past regrets to become obstacles to future growth. We can let go of outdated beliefs, behaviours, and limitations that may hold us back. This process requires courage and self-reflection as we confront our fears and insecurities. As we navigate the unknown, we learn valuable lessons about ourselves, gaining insights into our strengths, passions, and desires. We will discover "who" we are; our value and worth are priceless.

Embracing change also means embracing the discomfort that often accompanies it. Change can be unsettling and may push us beyond our familiar boundaries. However, we grow and develop through these moments of despair. We build resilience, adaptability, and confidence in overcoming obstacles by facing challenges head-on.

Taking on a healed identity after many years of defeat and hurt is a transformation that may take some time. It is a profound process when we consciously reshape and redefine our sense of self. It involves examining our core values, beliefs, and aspirations and aligning them with the person we want to become. Through this process, we can redefine ourselves to reflect our authentic selves.

Restructuring how we think requires self-awareness and introspection. It entails exploring our passions, interests, and values. It is understanding how they align with how we see ourselves and what we want for our future. It may involve shedding old personas or roles that no longer serve us and embracing new aspects of ourselves that resonate deeply.

Reconditioning our minds and restructuring what we think is not an overnight but a continuous journey. The more we become aware of our value and worth, the more persistent we will become.

Changes involve setting goals, making intentional choices, and taking consistent action toward personal growth and fulfillment. Along the way, we may encounter setbacks and challenges, which serve as opportunities for further development and self-discovery.

As we reshape our thinking, we unlock profound personal empowerment and fulfillment. We gain a renewed sense of purpose and clarity about our life's direction. By aligning our actions with our newly defined way of thinking, we live with integrity and authenticity, which fosters a deep sense of fulfillment and inner peace.

Ultimately, embracing change and reshaping our self-image allows us to tap into our full potential and live a life that is true to who we are. We were born to be champions. The value and worth we carry are priceless. No one can approve us but God.

We are empowered to create a meaningful life, contribute positively to those around us, and make a lasting impact in our world. Through this journey of appreciating ourselves, we discover our worth and value and inspire and uplift others to embark on their transformative paths.

We will come to a place where we refuse to allow our past to determine our future. We will refuse to let our abuse, traumas, negative upbringing, and emotional pain lead us. We will draw the line on the sand and put closure to the past. We will rebuild the broken bridge of trust, forgive those who may have hurt us and start with a new solid foundation. We will realize that we cannot change the past but can change the future. There is no need to cry over spilled milk; we cannot prevent the occurrence from happening, but we can avoid it.

# REBUILDING SELF-TRUST

**R**ecognizing the importance of rebuilding self-trust becomes crucial on the path to recovery. Without trust in ourselves, we may struggle to make decisions, assert our boundaries, and believe in our capabilities. Reestablishing trust in ourselves allows us to regain our sense of agency and reclaim our power.

One way to rebuild self-trust is by setting realistic goals and taking small steps toward achieving them. By breaking larger tasks into manageable milestones, we can build confidence in our ability to follow through and accomplish our goals. Each small achievement reinforces the belief that we are capable and trustworthy.

Honouring personal boundaries and needs is another essential aspect of cultivating self-trust. After experiencing trauma, our boundaries may have been violated, and we may have neglected our needs to appease others. By setting and enforcing limits that align with our values and well-being, we send a powerful message to ourselves that our needs matter and that we can trust ourselves to protect and care for ourselves.

Celebrating achievements, no matter how small, is essential in rebuilding self-trust. Taking the time to acknowledge and celebrate our successes helps to reinforce a positive self-image and fosters a sense of self-worth. No matter how seemingly insignificant, each achievement is a testament to our resilience and growth.

Learning from setbacks on the journey to rebuilding self-trust is equally important. Setbacks are an inevitable part of life, and experiencing them does not diminish our worth or abilities. Instead of viewing setbacks as failures, we can see them as opportunities for growth and learning. Reflecting on setbacks, identifying lessons, and adjusting our approach demonstrate that we can navigate challenges and adapt, reinforcing our self-trust in adversity.

Rebuilding self-trust after trauma requires patience, compassion, and perseverance. It is a process that may have its ups and downs, but each step taken toward trusting ourselves again is a step closer to personal growth and healing.

By setting realistic goals, honouring our boundaries and needs, celebrating achievements, and learning from setbacks, we can gradually rebuild our trust in ourselves. As we do so, we rediscover our inner strength and resilience, paving the way for a brighter, more empowered future.

In a world that often equates vulnerability with weakness, it is crucial to challenge societal perceptions and recognize the inherent strength that lies within vulnerability. Rather than viewing vulnerability as something to be avoided or concealed, it can be seen as a critical component of genuine connection and personal growth. When we allow ourselves to be vulnerable, we open the door to authentic and deep relationships with others and ourselves.

Understanding vulnerability requires a shift in perspective. It is not a sign of fragility or incompetence but a testament to our courage and resilience. After experiencing trauma, embracing vulnerability can be particularly challenging. The wounds we carry may make us hesitant to expose our emotions and innermost thoughts, fearing further harm or rejection. However, the seeds of growth and healing can be sown in these moments of fear and uncertainty.

To cultivate vulnerability, we must start with self-compassion and self-acceptance. It begins by recognizing that vulnerability is a natural part of the human experience and that we deserve love and understanding, regardless of our past traumas. By practicing self-compassion, we offer ourselves kindness and compassion, acknowledging our pain while refusing to let it define us.

Establishing trusting relationships is another crucial aspect of embracing vulnerability. Surrounding ourselves with individuals who create safe spaces and encourage open and honest communication allows us to let down our guard gradually. These relationships can provide support, empathy, and validation, reminding us that we are not alone in our struggles. As we share our vulnerabilities with trusted others, we begin to experience the power of genuine connection and the strength that emerges from it.

Engaging in creative outlets or therapeutic modalities that promote self-expression is another way to cultivate vulnerability. Art, music, writing, or creative expression can provide a safe space for exploring and processing our emotions. Through these mediums, we can voice our pain, hopes, and dreams, allowing our innermost selves to be seen and heard. Similarly, therapeutic modalities such as talk therapy or group therapy provide structured environments where vulnerability is accepted and actively encouraged. They offer opportunities to delve deeper into our experiences, share our stories, and receive support and guidance on our healing journey.

As we navigate the path of embracing vulnerability, it is essential to approach it with patience and self-care. Opening ourselves up to exposure can be uncomfortable and may trigger emotions we have long buried. Taking the time to practice self-care, engaging in activities that nourish our well-being, and seeking professional guidance are vital steps in this process.

Embracing vulnerability requires us to challenge societal narratives, recognize their strength, and summon the courage to be vulnerable after experiencing trauma. By cultivating self-compassion, establishing trusting relationships, and engaging in creative outlets or therapeutic modalities, we create space for growth, connection, and healing. Vulnerability is not a weakness to be shunned but a powerful tool for personal transformation and authentic connection with others. As we embrace vulnerability, we embark on a profound journey of self-discovery, resilience, and realizing our inherent worth and strength.

In the journey of healing and rebuilding after trauma, self-care is a crucial aspect that deserves our utmost attention. It is an essential component that allows us to nurture ourselves, regain strength, and restore balance. Recognizing the significance of self-care empowers us to prioritize our well-being, acknowledging that we deserve care and attention.

Self-care encompasses various dimensions, each vital in our overall healing process. The first dimension is physical self-care, which involves tending to our physical well-being. It includes activities such as maintaining a balanced diet, engaging in regular exercise or movement that feels good to our bodies, getting enough sleep, and addressing any physical ailments or discomforts. Taking care of our physical health provides a solid foundation for our emotional and mental well-being.

Emotional self-care is another dimension that requires our focus. It involves recognizing and honouring our emotions, allowing ourselves to feel and process them in a healthy and supportive way.

Emotional self-care can include engaging in therapy or counselling to work through emotional wounds, practicing mindfulness or meditation to cultivate emotional awareness, engaging in creative outlets like art or music to express emotions, or simply engaging in activities that bring us joy and uplift our spirits.

The mental dimension of self-care revolves around nurturing our cognitive well-being. It involves engaging in activities that stimulate and challenge our minds, fostering intellectual growth and resilience. This can include reading books or articles on topics of interest, learning new skills or hobbies, engaging in puzzles or brain exercises, or even seeking mental stimulation through conversations or debates. Taking care of our mental health enhances our cognitive abilities and contributes to a sense of fulfillment and purpose.

Lastly, the spiritual dimension of self-care recognizes the importance of nurturing our connection with something greater than ourselves. It involves exploring and cultivating our spiritual beliefs or practices, whatever they may be for each individual. This can include engaging in meditation or prayer, spending time in nature and connecting with the natural world, participating in religious or spiritual rituals, or seeking guidance from spiritual mentors or communities. Spiritual self-care provides a sense of solace, direction, and purpose, offering a space for reflection and inner peace.

Developing a personalized self-care routine is a powerful way to nurture ourselves on a deeper level. It involves carving out dedicated time and space to engage in activities that bring us joy, comfort, and rejuvenation. Building a self-care routine requires self-reflection and exploration of what truly nourishes and replenishes our spirit, body, and soul.

Consider starting by identifying activities that resonate with you. These simple pleasures bring you a sense of calm, happiness, or relaxation. It could be setting aside time each day for meditation or deep breathing exercises to center yourself. Perhaps you find solace and joy in journaling, where you can freely express your thoughts and emotions without judgment. Engaging with nature through walks in the park or gardening can offer a soothing connection with the natural world.

We must listen to our needs and preferences as we develop self-care routines. Experiment with different activities and pay attention to how they make us feel. Remember that self-care is a deeply personal practice, and what works for one person may not work for another. It is about finding what resonates with us and bringing it into our daily lives in an authentic and nurturing way.

Remember that self-nurturing is not a one-time event but an ongoing commitment to yourself. Incorporate self-care activities into your routine consistently, and be gentle with yourself when life gets busy or challenging. This helps you regain the value and worth you carry and not lose sight of your life is priceless.

In the face of adversity, stories of individuals who have overcome immense challenges can be powerful sources of inspiration. These stories highlight the human spirit's remarkable capacity to rise above even the most difficult circumstances. They remind us that resilience is not an abstract concept but a tangible quality that resides within each of us.

Resilient people often find a higher calling or a passion that fuels their drive to overcome challenges.

Whether through advocacy work, creative pursuits, or helping others, they channel their pain into something purposeful. They see purpose and value in others and appreciate themselves for not giving up. They know their worth and become passionate about sharing it with others.

Furthermore, a resilient individual develops a strong support network. They recognize the significance of surrounding themselves with people who believe in their potential, provide emotional support, and offer guidance. These relationships become pillars of strength, allowing them to navigate challenging times more resiliently.

When we immerse ourselves in resiliency, we tap into a wellspring of motivation and determination. We witness the triumph of the human spirit firsthand and realize that, despite our challenges, we can persevere. We use our resilient stories as a source of inspiration; we cultivate a positive mindset that empowers us to reframe challenges as opportunities for growth.

Instead of viewing setbacks as insurmountable obstacles, we see them as valuable lessons and stepping stones toward personal development. This shift in perspective allows us to approach challenges with resilience and an unwavering belief in our ability to overcome them.

Building resilience requires consistent effort and practice. Gratitude practices play a crucial role in this process, allowing us to focus on the positive aspects of our lives. By acknowledging and appreciating even the smallest blessings, we cultivate a sense of optimism and resilience. Additionally, incorporating positive affirmations into our daily routine helps rewire our thinking patterns, reinforcing self-belief and fortifying our strength.

Self-reflection becomes a valuable tool in fostering hope and perseverance. Examining our experiences, emotions, and growth allows us to recognize our resilience and progress. Through introspection, we gain insight into our strengths, resilience strategies, and areas for further development.

This self-awareness becomes a foundation upon which we can build resilience and face future challenges with renewed determination. It helps us to identify with our past and prevents the hurts and emotional wounds from stealing our concepts of the value and worth we carry. We can trust ourselves again and regain the positive mindset of the "who" we are and not the "who" we think we are. We see our value, worth, and the need to guard our hearts and minds, protecting our character from tarnishing. We see value even when broken, like the next chapter explains the concept of kintsugi.

# KINTSUGI

In the enchanting world of ancient Japan, there existed a significant art form known as Kintsugi. Passed down through generations, this art captured the essence of beauty in a truly extraordinary way. Imagine delicate pottery, once shattered and fragmented but restored to reveal a newfound splendour. Kintsugi, meaning "golden joinery," was the delicate art of repairing broken ceramics with gold or other precious metals.

As the sun cast its golden rays upon the broken pieces, skilled artisans would patiently mend the shattered pottery, employing their craftsmanship to transform it into something even more captivating. They would delicately apply the golden seams with meticulous care, tracing the fracture lines and embracing the imperfections. It was not an attempt to hide the damage but a celebration of the pottery's journey and a testament to its resilience.

The philosophy behind Kintsugi went far beyond mere physical restoration. It symbolized finding beauty in brokenness, embracing the flaws and cracks that told a story of endurance and growth. The gold that adorned the pottery's scars represented the preciousness and worthiness of the healing process. It was a reminder that something broken could be made whole again and become even more precious and unique in that process.

Kintsugi spoke to a profound truth that transcended pottery that touched the very fabric of our lives. It beckoned us to embrace our brokenness, to see our wounds as part of our journey rather than something to be hidden or ashamed of. It invited us to recognize that our scars, whether physical or emotional, contribute to the tapestry of our individuality and worth.

Through Kintsugi, we learn that it is in the mending of our broken pieces, in the acknowledgment of our cracks, that we discover a new sense of beauty and resilience. We understand that our vulnerabilities can be transformed into strengths and that our healing journey can be a remarkable testament to our worth. And just as the golden seams adorned the pottery, we, too, can embrace the golden threads that weave through our lives, illuminating our uniqueness and celebrating the beauty of embracing our brokenness.

You will marvelled at its inherent beauty as you hold the delicate piece of broken pottery in your hands. The cracks that snaked through its surface seemed to tell a story of resilience and transformation. It shows that nothing broken is worthless and that brokenness can give more value.

Kintsugi, the ancient Japanese art of repairing broken pottery with gold or other precious metals, represents a profound philosophy. It is finding beauty in brokenness and embracing imperfections. It celebrates the flaws and fractures that make an object unique rather than attempting to hide or discard them. It enhances value and worth.

Just like the pottery restored through Kintsugi, our lives are often marked by moments of brokenness. We face challenges, heartaches, and setbacks that leave us feeling fragmented and imperfect. Yet, in these very moments, a hidden beauty is waiting to be discovered. Our mistakes, flaws, regrets, and weaknesses can all be turned into something beautiful. Something priceless with value and worth that never tarnished.

The golden seams that run along the cracks of the repaired pottery are not intended to erase the past or cover up the damage. Instead, they serve as a testament to the journey of healing and growth. They highlight the scars and wounds that have been mended, transforming them into cherished reminders of strength and resilience.

In a world that often pressures us to strive for perfection and hide our vulnerabilities, Kintsugi reminds us of the inherent worth and beauty within our brokenness. It invites us to embrace our imperfections, recognizing that they contribute to our uniqueness and individuality.

Just as the repaired pottery becomes a work of art, we can find new purpose and meaning through our healing journey. We can see the beauty in our stories by acknowledging and accepting our cracks. We become a living embodiment of Kintsugi, showcasing the power of transformation and the strength that arises from embracing our brokenness.

Kintsugi teaches us that imperfection is not something to be ashamed of but rather a source of strength and resilience. It invites us to honour our visible and invisible scars and recognize the beauty that emerges when we choose to heal and grow.

In the golden threads that mend the broken pottery, we can see a reflection of our journey. It reminds us that the cracks in our lives do not diminish our worth but rather enhanced by the courage to face them head-on. With each healing step, we are repairing what was broken and crafting a unique story of resilience and self-acceptance.

Kintsugi teaches us that our brokenness does not define us but sets the stage for our most extraordinary transformations. It is a powerful reminder that there is beauty in every crack and strength waiting to be uncovered within ourselves.

Applying Kintsugi to our existence allows us to embrace a mindset of appreciation for our flaws and imperfections. Just as the skilled artisans of Kintsugi repair broken pottery with gold and other precious metals, we, too, can mend our shattered pieces with love and acceptance.

Instead of hiding or discarding our imperfections, we recognize their inherent beauty and value. We come to understand that it is through our cracks and scars that our uniqueness shines forth.

In adopting the mindset of Kintsugi, we shift our perspective. We no longer view our flaws as shortcomings but as badges of resilience and growth. We begin to see the intricate patterns our experiences form, each line telling a story of strength and transformation.

With this newfound appreciation for our brokenness, we can nurture a deep sense of self-compassion. We learn to be gentle with ourselves, understanding that we are all works in progress. We acknowledge that our imperfections do not diminish our worth but rather enhance it, adding depth and character to the masterpiece that is our life.

Applying Kintsugi to our lives requires a shift in our mindset and a willingness to embrace vulnerability. It invites us to let go of the pursuit of perfection and instead embrace the beauty that arises from embracing our authentic selves. Just as Kintsugi pottery becomes more valuable after being repaired, we, too, become more valuable as we welcome our flaws and allow ourselves to be seen in all our imperfect glory.

So, let us take inspiration from the art of Kintsugi and apply it to our own lives. Let us mend our broken pieces with the golden threads of self-acceptance and appreciation. In doing so, we can cultivate a deep sense of worth and value, recognizing that our cracks and imperfections are not flaws to be hidden but rather treasures to be celebrated.

We must explore our realities regarding who we are and avoid living in a fantasy world. We must face our existence and emotional wounds to regain ourselves and see our value and worth. We need to discover the "who" we are and learn to embrace it. We need to be able to look at ourselves in the mirror and feel comfortable in our skin.

When we can appreciate the Kintsugi of our souls, we can live life to its fullest. When we can love ourselves and be able to date the person we see in the mirror, we will not depend on others to fill our emptiness. We must see Kintsugi embracing our value and worth by discovering our true selves!

# SELF-DISCOVERY

L ife can throw us unexpected challenges, leaving us feeling overwhelmed and helpless. But in moments of crisis, we often discover an inner strength we never knew we had. This strength of self-discovery is within us; the ability to bounce back and overcome adversity. We need to discover our true selves and explore the power we carry.

We can start the healing journey by learning that tapping into our inner selves and discovering our true selves is okay. We need to first believe in ourselves before we can believe in others. We need to see that others can only add value to us but cannot make the choices we need to function.

We must recognize that setbacks and hardships are a natural part of life, and we have the power to rise above them. This requires a mindset shift from one of defeat to one of possibility and growth. We need to see reasons to move ahead, not losing sight of the value and worth we carry. Our lives can affect others in a positive nature once we discover our true selves. We have more in us that can impact others than we anticipate.

Once we can believe in ourselves, we can begin to nurture self-discovery. We can develop healthy coping mechanisms, such as meditation or exercise, to help us manage stress and anxiety. We can also build a support system of friends and family who can offer encouragement and guidance during tough times.

We must learn from our experiences and use them to grow stronger. Rather than dwelling on our failures or setbacks, we can reflect on what we learned and how to apply those lessons moving forward. With each challenge we overcome, we become more resilient and better equipped to face whatever comes next.

Life is a journey, and growth and self-discovery are essential to recognize our worth. The ups and downs we experience along the way are all opportunities for personal development, and we can learn valuable lessons from each.

Focusing solely on the result can be tempting, but honouring the process is essential. Every step we take, every challenge we overcome, and every setback we face is a testament to our value and worth. We can better understand ourselves and our values by embracing the journey and its ups and downs.

To truly embrace growth opportunities, viewing challenges and setbacks as chances for personal development is essential. Instead of getting bogged down by failures, regrets or mistakes, we can learn from them and use them as opportunities to become stronger. This requires a shift in perspective, but it can become second nature with practice.

Throughout the journey of self-discovery, patience and persistence are crucial. It's important to remember that personal growth is not a linear process, and there will be setbacks and obstacles along the way. By maintaining a culture of self-discovery, we can stay committed to our growth and learn to navigate the challenges that come our way.

In the end, it's the journey of growth and self-discovery that genuinely defines our worth. By embracing the process, viewing challenges as opportunities, and maintaining patience and persistence, we can continue to grow and thrive in all aspects of our lives.

In discovering our true worth, there is immense power in embracing self-acceptance. Through self-acceptance, we recognize and honour our inherent value, irrespective of our flaws or imperfections. When we look at ourselves with compassionate eyes, appreciating our uniqueness, we unlock a deep sense of self-worth.

One of the most significant barriers to self-acceptance is the habit of self-judgment. We often find ourselves caught in a cycle of negative self-talk and self-criticism, constantly highlighting our perceived shortcomings. We must consciously redirect our thoughts and replace self-judgment with self-compassion to challenge this damaging pattern.

By becoming aware of our negative self-talk, we can question its validity and challenge the harsh judgments we impose upon ourselves. Instead of focusing on our flaws, mistakes, and regrets, we can acknowledge our strengths, accomplishments, and the qualities that make us unique. Celebrating our progress, no matter how small can help us break free from the grip of self-judgment and foster a more positive and accepting mindset.

Practicing self-discovery is an essential component of cultivating self-acceptance. It involves treating ourselves with kindness, understanding, and unconditional love, just as we would extend to a dear friend or loved one facing challenges.

To practice self-discovery, we can offer ourselves words of kindness and encouragement. When faced with difficulties or setbacks, instead of criticizing ourselves, we can remind ourselves that mistakes and failures are natural parts of the human experience. Embracing self-discovery allows us to acknowledge our vulnerabilities, validate our emotions, and provide ourselves with the support we need to heal and grow.

By cultivating self-acceptance, challenging self-judgment, and practicing self-compassion, we can gradually transform our relationship with ourselves. We begin to see that our worth is not determined by external validations or the absence of flaws but rather by our ability to embrace and love ourselves, flaws and all. As we embark on this journey of self-acceptance, we unlock the true essence of our worth and radiate an inner beauty that shines brightly in the world.

In the captivating journey of self-discovery, a remarkable chapter unravels the significance of embracing uniqueness and celebrating individuality. Like the vibrant strokes of an artist's brush, our lives are painted with diverse colours, each representing our own set of qualities and strengths. We find the true essence of our worth within these distinct brushstrokes.

In a world often consumed by comparisons and conformity, embracing individuality becomes a powerful act of self-empowerment. By recognizing and appreciating the unique qualities that make us who we are, we pave the way for self-acceptance and personal growth. Whether it's our talents, perspectives, or quirks, each aspect of our individuality contributes to the tapestry of humanity, adding depth and richness to the world.

Yet, embracing our individuality goes beyond mere recognition; it requires the cultivation of authenticity. Authenticity is the courage to express ourselves genuinely without fear of judgment or rejection. It is the audacity to showcase our true selves to the world unabashedly and unapologetically. When we foster authenticity, we permit others to do the same, creating a vibrant tapestry of diverse identities, ideas, and contributions.

To truly celebrate our individuality, we must embark on a journey of self-discovery. It involves exploring our passions, values, and interests and aligning our lives with what truly resonates within us. It may require breaking free from societal expectations or relinquishing the need for external validation. This journey is not always easy, but it leads to a profound sense of fulfillment and an unwavering belief in our worth.

In embracing our uniqueness, we honour the mosaic of human existence. We become catalysts for change, inspiring others to discover and embrace their individuality. By bringing our authentic selves to the table, we contribute fresh perspectives, innovative ideas, and a rich tapestry of experiences that shape the world around us.

So, let us embark on this enchanting voyage, celebrating the beauty of our individuality and recognizing the immeasurable value it brings to the world. Let us stand tall, unafraid to paint our lives with the hues of our true selves. In doing so, we create a symphony of diverse voices, each contributing its melody, enriching the world with the brilliance of our uniqueness.

# HEIRLOOM

eirlooms hold a profound significance in our lives, transcending their material nature to become vessels of memories, stories, and emotions. They are not just objects but treasures connecting us to our past, roots, and the people who came before us. These cherished possessions carry the weight of history, bearing witness to our ancestors' triumphs, struggles, and journeys.

The sentimental value attached to heirlooms is immeasurable. They embody the love, devotion, and enduring bonds shared by generations. Each piece carries a unique story, passed down through time, from the hands of our grandparents, great-grandparents, or even further back. Whether it's a delicate piece of jewelry worn by a beloved grandmother or a weathered book filled with handwritten notes, these heirlooms evoke a tangible connection to those who have gone before us.

Beyond their physical presence, heirlooms undeniably emotionally impact individuals and families. They can evoke a range of emotions - joy, nostalgia, love, and sometimes even grief. The mere sight or touch of an heirloom can transport us to a different era, conjuring memories of laughter-filled family gatherings, intimate conversations by the fireplace, or the loving touch of a departed relative. They are tangible reminders of the shared experiences and enduring bonds that shape our identity.

In reflecting on the emotional impact of heirlooms, we understand that they carry not only the stories of our ancestors but also the essence of who we are as individuals and families. They serve as touchstones to our heritage, grounding us in belonging and continuity. Through heirlooms, we inherit material possessions and a rich tapestry of traditions, values, and wisdom that we are responsible for preserving and passing on to future generations.

As we explore the meaning of heirlooms, we understand their value and worth more profoundly. It is not solely measured by their monetary price or rarity but by the intangible treasures they hold. They are artifacts of love, resilience, and the enduring spirit of those who came before us. Heirlooms are bridges that span across time, connecting us to our ancestors, fostering a sense of belonging, and reminding us of the legacy we carry within us.

Heirlooms hold a remarkable power to carry the stories and values of our ancestors through the generations. They serve as tangible links to our past, embodying the experiences and memories of those who came before us. Each heirloom is a vessel of history, profoundly connecting us with our family's journey and heritage.

We are transported to a different time when we gaze upon an heirloom, be it a piece of jewelry, a handwritten letter, or an antique artifact. We can almost hear the whispers of our ancestors, feel their presence, and understand the significance of their lives. Heirlooms become more than mere objects; they become gateways to the past.

The role of heirlooms in preserving family history and heritage cannot be overstated. They serve as repositories of memories, capturing the essence of our family's triumphs, struggles, and traditions. Through heirlooms, we can piece together narratives that might have otherwise been lost to time, uncovering stories that shape our understanding of who we are and where we come from.

Moreover, heirlooms are vital in nurturing our sense of ancestral identity. They connect us to our roots and provide a tangible link to our lineage. As we hold a treasured heirloom, we feel a deep connection to the individuals who cherished it before us, weaving together a tapestry of shared experiences and values. In this way, heirlooms become touchstones that ground us, reminding us of the legacy we inherit and the responsibility we have to preserve it.

Preserving family legacy through heirlooms is not merely an act of conservation but a profound act of reverence. We honour our forebears' sacrifices, achievements, and lessons by safeguarding these precious artifacts. We pass on their legacy to future generations, ensuring that the stories and values they held dear continue to resonate through time.

In this age of rapid change and fleeting moments, heirlooms serve as steady anchors, reminding us of the enduring nature of our family's legacy. They remind us of the importance of our heritage, urging us to cherish and protect the treasures that bind us to the past. As custodians of our family's legacy, we have the privilege and responsibility to ensure that heirlooms continue to carry forward the stories and values that shape our identity.

Heirlooms hold a profound and intangible power—the ability to evoke strong emotional attachments and memories within individuals and families. The stories of those who came before we lie within the intricate details and worn surfaces, allowing us to connect on a deeper level with our ancestors. Through these treasured objects, we glimpse into their lives, the joys they celebrated, and the adversities they endured.

The psychological impact of heirlooms is undeniable. In a world that often seems temporary and transient, heirlooms offer a sense of permanence—a reminder that we are part of a greater narrative connected to a lineage that stretches far beyond our existence.

Moreover, heirlooms have a unique ability to foster emotional bonds and connections between family members. As we gather, passing an heirloom from one generation to the next, we create a tangible thread that weaves our stories together. Sharing the narratives and memories associated with these precious objects becomes an act of love and intimacy as we pass down the physical heirloom and the emotions and connections it represents.

The presence of heirlooms in our lives encourages dialogue and fosters a sense of belonging. Whether retelling the tale of a precious family heirloom or reminiscing about the loved ones who once cherished it, these conversations strengthen the bonds between generations. The stories embedded within heirlooms become a shared heritage, creating a bridge that spans time and reinforces the ties that bind us.

In these conversations, some may see the value of the heirloom they carry and the value and worth of the person who owned it. We must remind ourselves that those who could pass on an heirloom had struggles, mistakes, weaknesses, and regrets, just like we do. They were able to pass something physical down that was priceless. However, most importantly, they could pass down 'some of themselves' with it, making the physical object invaluable.

In a world where material possessions often lose their lustre with time, heirlooms possess a rare quality—a value that transcends monetary worth. They remind us that our history is not confined to dusty pages in a forgotten book but lives on in the tangible artifacts passed down through the generations. Through our emotional connections to these heirlooms, we honour our ancestors, keep their memories alive, and strengthen the ties that bind us to our roots. Our ancestor's persistence in not giving up; their resiliency to keep moving ahead created a priceless heirloom.

This is a life lesson regarding never giving up and not allowing our past to determine our future. We need to leave a legacy behind, an heirloom of something physical, but more so our spirit of what we did. We want to go something more than just with sentimental value.

We want to leave a wealth of wisdom and life lessons, transmitting knowledge and importance to the next generation.

We want to carry a unique narrative that encapsulates our experiences, struggles, and triumphs to those after us. It is through our stories that wisdom is embedded in heirlooms, waiting to be unravelled and cherished. We should want to leave material value and the intangible knowledge we hold.

Imagine running your fingers along the delicate embroidery of your great-grandmother's wedding veil, feeling a connection to her in a way that transcends time. At that moment, you are touching a piece of fabric and connecting with the wisdom of enduring love, commitment, and resilience. The heirloom becomes a tangible reminder of the enduring values that guided your ancestors, offering insights into the essence of a meaningful life.

We should want to link our heritage, preserving ancestral wisdom that might otherwise be lost in the ebb and flow of time. We must embody the traditions, customs, and beliefs to pass them on to our children, grandchildren, and hopefully great-grandchildren. It's a continuity and identity. Through our experiences, we can glimpse life's lessons learned, serving as guideposts to the next generation.

The importance of preserving our experiences and wisdom cannot be overstated. They serve as touchstones that connect our children, grandchildren and the heritage left behind. We want the value and worth we embrace to be passed on to the next generation and the principles that have shaped our journey. By passing down these heirlooms to future generations, we ensure that the accumulated wisdom of our ancestors continues to resonate, inspiring and guiding those who come after us.

As we reflect on the significance of heirlooms in preserving experience and wisdom, we should be reminded of our role of appreciating our value and worth. We should never negate our past and use our regrets as reasons to lose sight of the value and worth we carry. We have something to live for; we want to history our life's story to give someone hope to keep living and never to give up. This is the light at the end of every tunnel. There is water in every hole dug. Never stop pursuing happiness.

It is our responsibility to cherish and protect our failures and accomplishments and share the stories and lessons they hold. Engaging in conversations and passing on the associated narratives can create a bridge between generations, fostering a sense of interconnectedness and a deeper understanding of our shared legacy.

Ultimately, our heirlooms will not just be physical objects; they will be vessels of wisdom, carriers of values, and beacons of our collective history. They will remind others of the journeys undertaken, the challenges we faced, and the knowledge we acquired along the way. Through the preservation and transmission of our experience and wisdom embedded in our heirlooms, we will ensure that the timeless lessons of our past continue to shape and inspire the future.

When our heirlooms are brought out, they can radiate an aura of history and continuity. They can remind us of our past and anchor for the present, connecting different generations through shared experiences. Moreover, our heirlooms will have the power to evoke stories and anecdotes of family traditions. As family members gather, our stories can unfold, intertwining the past with the present and imparting wisdom and life lessons to younger generations.

By cherishing our value and worth, families will honour our heritage and foster a sense of belonging and identity. They will serve as tangible reminders of never giving up. They provide a sense of continuity and stability in an ever-changing world, grounding the next generation in their roots, inspiring a sense of pride, and never giving up.

# CONCLUSION

In conclusion, we have learned through this book how important it is to value our value and worth. The need to have a sense of self-worth is essential in valuing ourselves, and having a sense of self-value is crucial to see our worthiness. When we value ourselves, we set higher expectations, building our self-esteem.

We have learned that we need to believe in ourselves and see our value and worth. Self-esteem is a sign that we are appreciating ourselves. Our confidence level will rise, and our insecurities will wither away. We need to be confident in the "who" we are to have excellent relationships with ourselves and others. Positive self-esteem is a sign that you are valuing the value and worth you have.

## CONCLUSION

We need to see ourselves as our best friends, our peers. In the same way, we would treat others with dignity and respect; we need to treat ourselves. Appreciate your skills, experience, and knowledge. Avoid seeing yourself as a supplicant. You need to feel privileged to be with yourself. Valuing yourself takes changing your thoughts and learning to let go of the past.

You know you value yourself when making a difference in the lives of your family, friends, colleagues and community. You don't allow what others say affects the "who" you are. You should never feel self-conscious around others; avoid people, places and situations because you feel insecure. You don't need to be validated or approved by others. You have to support yourself, and no need for constant reassurance. No need to be a people-pleaser, overly sensitive or fearful of others. Your confidence level shows you've accepted your value and worth.

We can all rebuild our self-value and self-worth by being committed, recognizing our strengths and weaknesses and dedicating ourselves to positive changes. We can focus on improving our perfectionism, not to be OCD driven, but to make sure we make the right choices and do things to the best of our abilities. We refrain from toxic relationships and invest in what can grow our value and worth.

We have learned how to use our past to fertilize our future; we can turn around our failures, weaknesses, mistakes, flaws, and regrets. Our past can catapult us into a bright future. We need to spend time celebrating, dating ourselves, and learning how to love the "who" we are, so we don't depend on others to fill the emptiness when love is missing in our hearts. Empathy carries a power which needs to be generated from ourselves and others. The power of empathy plays a significant role in building our confidence level and appreciating our value and worth.

The book helped us to understand that our hurt, abuse and traumas do not determine our future. We need to put closure to emotional wounds to move ahead. This will help us find our identity and positive self-image of ourselves. When we rebuild self-trust, we can gain much more than we can count on our fingers. Self-trust helps us to appreciate where we came from and where we don't want to go.

We learned about Kintsugi and how our cracks and brokenness give us more value and worth. Nothing is useless. Our brokenness is valuable, and we have to see it. When we discover ourselves and see ourselves are heirlooms we are pasting on to another generation, our self-value and self-worth become priceless.

I hope you enjoyed the book as much as I wanted to write it. The goal was to enlighten the readers to appreciate themselves and others. We cannot change our past, but we can change our future!!!

The end!

www.ingramcontent.com/pod-product-compliance
Lightning Source LLC
Chambersburg PA
CBHW011745020426
42333CB00022B/2719